kidscape
Help With Bullying

INTRODUCTION

This guide has been written to support you with bullying and relationships so you can feel happy and safe in school, the community and online. There is a section at the back that you can also share with your parent or carer.

For further advice visit www.kidscape.org.uk

CONTENTS

BULLYING

What is bullying?

Bullying is when one person or a group of people deliberately hurt another person, more than once. Sometimes we use STOP to help spot a bullying situation (Several Times on Purpose).

Bullying can be....

Verbal – name calling, unkind comments, spreading rumours, laughing at someone, forcing someone to do or say something, encouraging someone to hurt themselves

Physical – hitting, kicking, shoving, spitting, burning, touching us anywhere we do not want to be touched

Emotional – leaving someone out, unfriending, pressurising someone

Online – messages, posts, videos that are intended to hurt or cause harm, pretending to be someone else

It is often targeted at perceived 'difference' and may be driven by prejudice and harmful attitudes towards others. For example, bullying behaviour can be targeted at someone's race, faith, disability, sexuality, gender, age, appearance and social status. If you are bullied, it is never your fault. It is the person or people doing the bullying that needs to change their behaviour.

Remember: If you are bullied, it is NEVER your fault.

YOUR QUESTIONS ABOUT BULLYING - ANSWERED

1

Is bullying against the law?

Different countries will have different laws and legislation relating to bullying behaviour. At the current time there is no specific law against bullying in the United Kingdom, but all schools have a legal duty to keep children safe from bullying and harm, and some bullying behaviour may be criminal (for example, if someone physically or sexually assaults another person or threatens to cause them harm).

2

What is the difference between bullying and friendship fallouts?

Fallouts and conflict can happen in all relationships. This becomes bullying behaviour when someone uses their power to force someone else to agree with them, if they keep picking a fight with the same person, or if they encourage other people to join in.

3

What is the difference between bullying and teasing?

Teasing (sometimes called 'banter') between friends can be fun, when everyone is in on the joke and enjoying themselves.

It can move into bullying when someone is upset, hurt or offended, and the other person refuses to stop. For example, if someone keeps teasing you about something even if is clear it upsets you.

Teasing can also become bullying (and potentially harassment) when it is targeted at certain characteristics. For example, someone's skin colour, ethnic background, religion, sexuality or gender. You may feel under pressure to laugh, but these types of comments or jokes (even if you are not personally offended), create an environment where others may not feel safe, and bullying is more likely to happen.

4

Why do people bully others?

People bully others because they want to feel powerful and in control.

They may do it to feel more popular (for example, by making other people laugh or getting other people to be on their side) or to stop getting hurt themselves (for example, "If I hurt other people, no one can hurt me").

It can also be because:
- They find it hard to manage their own feelings and actions (for example, they often say hurtful things and hurt others)
- They have been bullied themselves
- They are experiencing violence at home
- They are jealous of other people
- They feel like they are not good enough
- They have negative beliefs about people who are different
- They are experiencing high levels of stress and anxiety.

WHAT CAN I DO IF I AM BEING BULLIED?

Research in the United Kingdom suggests at least 4 in 10 children will experience bullying in a year. This means nearly half of all children experience bullying at some point. You are not alone.

Anyone can be bullied and if it happens to you, you need to get help.

1) Tell someone you trust

Ask for their help to come up with a plan so the bullying stops. This may be a family member, a friend, a teacher from your school, or an adult in the community. Tell them how long it has been going on, who has been involved and how it makes you feel. If you are very nervous, write it down or record a video where you talk through what is happening, or ask a friend or family member to help you.

2) Report the bullying situation to the school

You can either report directly to your teacher or have your parents or carers do so on your behalf. It is the school's responsibility to keep you safe from bullying, so there will be procedures in place to support you. It will help the school if you can share what has happened, with who, and the impact it is having. You can also suggest actions that may help. You may want to keep a diary of events that you can share with the school.

3) Talk to a friend

Surrounding yourself with good friends is one of the best ways to prevent bullying. If you already have a group of friends that you like and trust, that is great. Ask for their help. We have advice later in this book on how to make friends.

4) Learn assertiveness skills

Assertiveness skills are when you feel strong and calm and can show that to others. For example, sitting or standing up tall, and using a firm calm voice with other people. Using assertiveness skills in a bullying situation can make a big difference, as you are standing up for yourself, showing that you respect yourself and others equally, and that you will not let the situation continue.

5) Always put your safety first

If someone has hurt you, or is threatening to hurt you, then get help. Get out of the situation as soon as you can. Look for an adult who can help and find a safe place. Contact the Police.

LEARNING MORE ABOUT ASSERTIVE SKILLS

You can be assertive with your voice and your body. It is a superpower we can all learn over time with a bit of support, even if we find communication difficult.

There are three styles of communication:

Passive
Behaving like someone else's rights matter more than yours.

Aggressive
Behaving like your rights matter more than someone else's.

Assertive
Behaving like your rights matter equally.

Bullying behaviour can take us all by surprise, and we may respond by being passive or aggressive. When bullying others, people are nearly always being aggressive.

Assertive: Behaving like your rights matter equally.

Your assertive voice

Your assertive voice is one that sounds strong, calm, and confident. Take a deep breath before speaking and do not let others rush you. You may want to practice in front of a mirror.

Start by practicing saying "no"
It is a short word, and it is a very useful one when someone is pressuring you to do something you don't want to do, or when someone is doing something and you'd like them to stop. Say it with strength in your voice, clearly, and loud enough to be heard.

Have some backup phrases
Once you're getting good at saying "no", try other phrases to stop bullying behaviour in its tracks, for example "that's mine, you can't have it", or "stop now – I don't like it". Sometimes in a bullying situation you might need to repeat yourself. Keep saying the same thing again in your assertive voice until they get the message!

Fog it out
If someone is saying an insulting comment, picture a protective fog around you that swallows up the words before they get to you. Your fog can be anything: some people imagine an animal, others a blanket, and others a marshmallow fortress – pick something that makes you feel safe. As your fog catches the bad words, acknowledge the comment with something like "that's your opinion" or "you noticed".

Assertive body language

Your body communicates more than your voice, so back up your assertive voice with assertive body language.

Hold your body in a way that makes you feel strong and powerful. Practice a "power pose" at home to help you get a feel for it. Hold your head high and relax your shoulders.

Make and maintain eye contact.
If eye contact is difficult for you, try looking at the tops of someone's ears or in between their eyes!

Fake it till you make it!
You might not start to feel more confident immediately, but you will look it. It will soon start to come naturally to you.

The power of music
It can even help if you're going into a difficult situation - whether at work, school or home - to listen to music that helps you feel strong and powerful.

Practicing assertiveness

Using your assertive voice and body language helps you respond to bullying in a safe and effective way. Communication skills are a life skill, taking time and practice. To help it come more easily, try practicing somewhere you feel safe, with someone you trust.

Mirror practice
Get in front of the mirror and practice your body language and voice.

The human mirror
Ask a trusted friend or family member to mirror your body language. How do you think they appear? If they are not looking assertive, try shifting your body language.

Look at characters on TV or in films
Watch their body language and their voices. Are they being passive, aggressive, or assertive?

Role playing
Ask a trusted friend or family member to role play scenarios with you. Think about what a bully might say to you and try out your assertive responses. Return the favour and help them be more assertive, too!

Practice with Kidscape
Children in England and Wales can access Kidscape ZAP workshops that help you explore and unlock assertiveness in a safe setting with other young people who have experienced bullying. For more information visit the Kidscape website.

Be assertive as much as you can, not just when you are being bullied. Showing the world that you respect yourself and others is something you can do all the time - and the more you practice it, the easier it comes. For example, when was the last time you told a friend or family member that as much as love them, what they said upset you? Always stand up for yourself, and eventually, it will be part of your life!

WHAT CAN I DO IF I AM BEING BULLIED ON THE JOURNEY TO OR FROM SCHOOL OR IN THE WIDER COMMUNITY?

You have a right to be safe from bullying wherever you are. This includes on the journey to and from school, in clubs and in the wider community.

Bullying on a school journey or in the wider community might include things like name calling, being pushed around, tripped over, hit and hurt, sexual comments or touching, having your belongings taken or destroyed, people taking photos or videos of you in order to make fun of you, or being forced to hand over money.

Bullying behaviour may be a criminal act if you are physically or sexually assaulted or threatened – whether face to face or through mobile phones. This means you can contact the police or your local authority for help.

If you are in immediate danger, then do what you can to get out of the situation and get help. If that means getting off the bus early, running to a safe place, yelling, or asking someone in a shop, or on the bus or train to help you, then do it. If you, or someone around you is at risk of being seriously hurt then contact the Police.

If you are being bullied, or you see it happening to other children then it is important you get help. Follow the steps above for what to do if you are being bullied – tell someone what is happening. If the bullying is in a club, they will also have a legal duty to keep you safe from all forms of bullying or harm.

In the short term do what you can to stay away from the people doing the bullying. Sit, stand, or travel to school with people you trust. If they are calling you names remember that there is nothing wrong with you. It is the people doing the bullying that have the problem, not you. It can help to repeat a sentence in your head that makes you feel safe or strong. For example, "I am not alone. I am stronger than this and will get through it."

Look out for other children that might be being bullied. Sit, stand, or walk with them.

You will need to decide whether it is safe to say something to children that are bullying or hurting others but make sure they can see you are not joining in or finding it funny. Let the school know if bullying is happening and ask what you can do together to make it stop.

Keep a diary of events. It can help the school or police if you keep a record of when and what is happening.

Bullying can make you feel sad, anxious, scared, and lonely. That is totally understandable, but you are not alone.

WHAT IF I AM BEING BULLIED ONLINE?

There can be a lot of negative behaviour online, and at some point, it is likely that we will all experience or see bullying or trolling. Online behaviour turns into bullying (or 'cyberbullying') when it is deliberate, it is repeated, and it is having a negative impact on how we feel. Here are some ways you can handle online bullying:

1) Try not to respond
The person wants a reaction and the less you give the more likely they are to move on. Be like an 'ice mountain' where you give them no footholds and they slide off!

2) If you do not know the person, unfriend or block them from your account
If you know them and you do not want to take that action, you can sometimes mute the person or the comments to give you a break. It can also help to go and do something else you enjoy for a while – such as playing a sport or watching a film. Distract yourself rather than going back to the messages.

3) If you know the person and it feels safe...
... you may want to contact them away from the platform to ask them to remove the comments or posts. Sometimes people are not aware of how they have made you feel.

4) Get help
If the situation continues, follow the other advice in this guide and get help from someone you trust. It can be helpful to keep evidence of what has happened – such as screen grabs. Schools should take online bullying seriously - particularly if it involves children from your school or is impacting how you feel during the school day.

5) Know when to contact the police

If someone is threatening you with harm, is encouraging you to harm yourself, has shared private images of you, or is using hate speech against you (like targeting your race, faith, sexuality, age, disability or gender) then contact the police.

6) Who else can help

Different countries will have different organisations who can support. In the United Kingdom, If you are under 18 you can also contact Report Harmful Content who assist with cyberbullying issues and removing harmful content: reportharmfulcontent.com/.

Are there ways to keep myself safe online so that bullying is less likely to happen?

While we are not in control of what others do or say, there are ways we can help to protect ourselves:

- Set the highest levels of privacy on your online accounts to protect who can see your information.
- Do not share your passwords with anyone.
- Consider limiting your friends and followers to people you know and trust.
- Think before you post – be careful not to respond to posts when you are feeling tired or angry.
- When you are sharing personal information about yourself keep in mind that you will not be able to control how others respond. It may be better to share big worries or concerns offline with a friend or family member.
- Remember you are worth more than a social media post! Sometimes we put ourselves under pressure to be popular online and to have lots of likes but this does not determine our worth. It is better to have a few good friends who truly know us and love us than lots of followers who only see a small part of our lives.

WHAT CAN I DO IF I SEE SOMEONE BEING BULLIED?

Most children do not bully and hurt other people. It is vital therefore that we all learn to be upstanders, protecting others when we spot a bullying situation - whether face to face or online. Here are some key actions you can take to be an upstander:

GET HELP

If you know that someone is being bullied, talk to a parent or teacher. If someone is being physically hurt, get help straight away. If you see bullying happening online, do not join in, and let the person experiencing the bullying know you are there for them.

STAND UP FOR THE PERSON BEING BULLIED

It takes courage, but next time you see someone say or do something to hurt someone else, make it clear you do not agree. If you feel unsafe doing this, ask for the support of your friends.

BE A FRIEND

Make a special effort to be kind to the person being bullied. Ask them to join your group, sit with them at lunchtime and include them in activities both within class and socially. You can even send them a message to say you are thinking of them.

NEVER JOIN IN

If you see someone being bullied, do not join in. If the person doing the bullying tries to draw you in, walk away or change the subject.

STOP THE RUMOURS

Don't help to spread rumours about another person. If someone fills you in on gossip, let it end with you.

DON'T BE AN INTERNET TROLL!

If there are rumours, offensive comments and pictures being spread on social media or on an internet site, do not add to it or share the posts further.

SUPPORT AND EMPOWER THE TARGET

Talk to the person being bullied. Try to offer them support and encourage them to report what is happening to the school. Tell them about Kidscape's website and offer to go with them to talk to a teacher or a trusted adult.

I AM WORRIED I MIGHT HAVE BULLIED OTHER PEOPLE. WHAT CAN I DO?

We all make mistakes and hurt other people. We may even have bullied others or got caught up in a bullying situation. If you have hurt someone, or got involved in a bullying situation, it is important to take the following actions:

1) Understand that bullying behaviour can cause serious harm.

2) Recognise when you have hurt someone else, or your behaviour has gone too far.

3) Stop. Stop saying or doing things that hurt other people. If you can, say sorry and do what you can to make the situation better.

4) Ask for help. If you find it hard not to say or do things that hurt others, or if you are hurting yourself, then ask for help.

RELATIONSHIPS

How can I handle peer pressure?

We all face pressure from other people – the people with the most influence over us are usually our friends, family, and classmates. It is an important skill to learn to 'stand up for yourself'. This means knowing what matters to you (your values), what you will and won't do (your boundaries), and how to use your assertiveness skills to manage any situation where you feel under pressure.

Your values are unique to you and help guide the decisions you make. Look at this list of words and circle those that mean the most to you. You may even want to add your own! Whenever you feel under pressure, think about whether you are acting according to your own values, or being pressured to be someone you're not!

ACCEPTANCE	CURIOSITY	GROWTH	PEACE
ACHIEVEMENT	DISCOVERY	HAPPINESS	PERFORMANCE
ASSERTIVENESS	ENERGY	HARD WORK	POWER
BALANCE	ENJOYMENT	HEALTH	RESPECT
BEAUTY	ENTHUSIASM	HONESTY	SKILL
BRAVERY	EQUALITY	HOPE	SMART
CALM	EXCELLENCE	IMAGINATION	SUCCESS
CERTAINTY	EXPERIENCE	INDIVIDUALITY	SUPPORT
CHALLENGE	FAMILY	INSPIRING	TALENT
CLEVER	FEARLESS	INTELLIGENCE	TEAMWORK
COMMUNITY	FEELINGS	JOY	THANKFUL
COMPASSION	FREEDOM	JUSTICE	TOUGHNESS
CONFIDENCE	FRIENDSHIP	KINDNESS	TRUST
CONNECTION	FUN	LEARNING	UNIQUENESS
CREATIVTY	GENEROSITY	LOVE	WEALTH
CREDIBILITY	GENIUS	LOYALTY	
	GIVING		

Practice using your assertiveness skills to say calmly and firmly 'no' to someone putting you under pressure. It can also help to give yourself time to consider a situation and the action you want to take. For example, say that you need time to think about it, then ask people you trust what they would do in the same situation.

How do I make friends?

It is important for all of us to have friends; people who care about us and make us smile. Whether you are feeling lonely, starting a new school or just open to exploring new friendships, here is some tips for making new friends:

MEET OTHER PEOPLE

Joining a club, youth group or getting involved in an activity you enjoy is a great way of meeting new people. It is also a boost to your confidence to do something you love! Do some research about what is available in your area and choose something that interests you. If you are unsure of where to start, ask someone to help you, or ask others for ideas.

SHOW YOU ARE OPEN WITH YOUR BODY LANGUAGE

If you look like you are trying to make yourself as small as possible, or you look threatening, people might not want to talk to you. Our tips on being assertive can help you practice your body language to show others that you're open to talking and friendship.

BE A GREAT LISTENER

Introduce yourself to new people, ask questions about them, really listen to their answers, and look for common ground.

HELP OTHER PEOPLE

Volunteering in your local community can be a great way to meet other people.

MAKE AN EFFORT

Do not wait for others to arrange something. Ask your new friends if they would like to hang out! Invite them to take part in activities with you.

BE A GOOD FRIEND

Be a good friend to your new friends. Be trustworthy, listen to them, be respectful and supportive. Read Kidscape's "What makes a good friend" guide for tips on good friendships.

CHOOSE GOOD FRIENDS

Most importantly, you deserve good friends. Surround yourself with people who make you feel good, and do not pursue friendships with people who do not.

How do I spot a frenemy?

Sometimes people who claim to be your friends can show bullying behaviour. These are sometimes called a 'frenemy' or 'frenemies'.

- They might say "brutally honest" things to you which are unkind or hurtful
- Put pressure on you to do things you do not want to do
- Be manipulative (such as "If you were my friend, you would…")
- Put you down
- Laugh at you, or encourage others to laugh at you
- Talk about you behind your back
- Deliberately exclude you from group chat and activities
- Take the "banter" too far
- Share things about you online
- Make you feel bad about yourself

This is not the sign of true friendship, and you may want to think carefully about ending the friendship, making new friends, or gradually spending less time with the person or people.

Frenemies are people that claim to be your friend but who show bullying behaviour.

How can I feel better if a friendship has ended?

It really hurts when a good friendship comes to an end. It is okay not to feel okay, and it is okay to miss the other person, and take time to feel better again. Here are some actions you can take:

Accept that not all relationships last forever
Think about everything good you can take away from your time together and what the relationship has taught you about yourself.

Accept that the relationship is different and move on
Do not try to force someone to be your friend or be unkind to someone who is no longer your friend. Make sure you do not share private information about the other person or encourage others not to be their friend.

Look to the future
You will make new friends. Smile knowing you had good times together, but that good times with other people lie ahead. Hold your head high, be kind, and be open to new friendships.

How can I help stop an argument?

We all get into arguments from time to time or may be a bystander when others are having an argument. It is important to learn how to quickly resolve arguments, so they do not turn into bullying situations.

1) Stop feeling like you must be right. There are no winners or losers, just different points of view.
2) Change the subject. Sometimes the best thing you can do is to agree to disagree and change the subject.
3) Take some time out. It may be better for everybody if you agree to all take some time out until you feel calmer, then come back together once you are ready to talk.
4) Do not encourage other people to argue or fight. Instead, encourage them to walk away, play a different game, or have a different conversation. If the debate is happening online, do not reshare or comment. It may be better to leave the conversation and come back at another time once things have calmed down.

WHO ELSE CAN HELP?

It is important to think about the different people in your life who may be able to give you support and advice in a bullying situation. This may be someone in your family, a parent or carer, a friend, or another adult you trust. If you are from the United Kingdom, the following organisations can give support:

Kidscape - www.kidscape.org.uk
Childline - www.childline.org.uk
The Mix - www.themix.org.uk
Ditch the Label - www.ditchthelabel.org

ADVICE FOR PARENTS AND CARERS

If your child is going through a bullying situation and you need help or advice, Kidscape is here for you. Kidscape is a bullying prevention charity working across England and Wales, which supports hundreds of families and thousands of children each year. We have lots of information and advice on our website, and we run free ZAP assertiveness workshops for children and families, as well as a Parent Advice Line. For more details visit www.kidscape.org.uk.

For more information...

You can find more information about our work on our website and via our highly active social media channels:

🌐 kidscape.org   f Kidscape Charity

 @Kidscape   ▶ Kidscape

 @Kidscape   in Kidscape

About Kidscape

Kidscape is a bullying prevention charity operating in England and Wales (registered number 326864), founded in 1985.

Our work includes online advice and resources, a parent advice line, and face-to-face workshops for children and families that build awareness and resilience, delivered both in schools and the community.

Printed in Great Britain
by Amazon

18697677R00016